WHOLESOME
IS OUR PRECIOUS
GENDER DIVIDE

PANTHEISTIC
POLITICAL
PHILOSOPHY

The Forgotten but complementary division
between the masculine and the feminine
phenomenon in all possible realms of life

ALEXANDER BARRIE

Physician of Natural Medicine

ISBN
978-1-958690-05-5 (Paperback)
978-1-958690-06-2 (eBook)
978-1-958690-04-8 (Hardcover)

TABLE OF CONTENTS

WHOLESOME IS OUR PRECIOUS GENDER DIVIDE

THE FORGOTTEN BUT COMPLEMENTARY DIVISION
BETWEEN THE MASCULINE AND THE FEMININE
PHENOMENON IN ALL POSSIBLE REALMS OF LIFE

In the majority of cases with us men-folk, with few exceptions, we would be content living inside caves as troglodytes, but for the female aspirations of the women-folk, and also, as the dictates of the feminine side of our own inner nature may direct us as men-folk.

Women naturally seek order, regulation and cleanliness. Confidentially, there are many humans around us who consider it a badge of honour to behave and to look like the troglodytes - where ever they are!

I am reminded of a little story told to me some forty years ago, of a young twenty five year-old man reaching a dramatic cross-roads in his life, and his confusion as to which path he should choose to make something of his present but difficult incarnation.

He was fortunate enough to gain an audience with a famous and highly respected lady Guru from India visiting London at they time. She suggested, in plain terms, when he spoke to her about himself and his life's-dilemma, to do four things: One - get a haircut. Two - get a shave. Three - take a bath. Four - find a job, any job!

Thomas Moore (1779-1852): "Disguise our bondage as we will....'tis woman, woman rules us still"

PREFACE & APOLOGIA:

The following texts should not be read as a criticism of English Speaking Peoples' who already possess many redeeming qualities. Nor are the following writings meant to be a debasing of our beautiful and expressive language of English in its richness (see later pages on gender in language value).

This Book conveys observations and hypotheses put forward for consideration and debate. In addition, some statements may not be entirely accurate in detail; what matters is the acknowledgement of a Male and of a Female division (sometimes referred-to as the Positive and the Negative) within the whole of creation.

I pray that the contents of these writings offend no one person, and that they are taken as thought-provoking ideas.

PROLOGUE

Those things which are manifest - that is: in matter, form, in the way of material and tangible objects as in fauna, flora, and minerals and also notions that gain actual substance because they have physically come into being: may all be deemed as Feminine in nature. They possess the force that is gravitationally centripetal. We are talking support and structure here, the giving of nourishment to innervate life - these concerns are about ramification and detail.

The un-manifested, is that which is hidden, invisible and is therefore abstract in nature rather than that which is in evidence and in concretion. The un-manifested is an energetic creative force that is behind, beneath, above, within, and in fact all round and ordered by a Supreme Intelligence. This Supreme Intelligence may be deemed Masculine in nature and represents the wider universal vista. This wider universal vista, because its force is centrifugal in nature and therefore rarefied, is The Source of All and Everything. We are speaking about the idea and the plan (Male - centrifugal) in the abstract before its material reflection (Female - centripetal) comes into being.

For many of us this philosophy is a little difficult to comprehend, but may be perceived as truth at curious moments when we are fortunate enough to experience a relevant Revelation and with this very personal experience, possibly an Epiphany.

The Ancients considered all that is of Earth is Female and factual, and all that is of Heaven is Male and conceptual.

Heaven attracts Earth and Earth attracts Heaven each with a compulsive power to unite, almost beyond comprehension. This Law of Attraction is a useful guide for the arguments put forward below and is explained more exhaustively as the contents of this Book develop.

AN ADDITIONAL KEY TO MAKE SENSE OF THE FOLLOWING TEXTS:

The hidden, the un-manifested aspects of life that are deemed the Masculine forces of Heaven with their rarefaction, and the manifested, with their tangible aspects of life deemed the Female forces of Earth and their concretion, is the recipe required to understand the nature of this difficult Work:

Consider Heaven's potential splendour and radiance and all that it contains and from which issues TRUTH (Masculine); but from the point of view of Earth's inherent appetite for tangibles: PROOF (Feminine) is required to verify the TRUTH !

In common parlance: "To walk the talk". The theme of TRUTH (Male), but show me the PROOF (Female) of the TRUTH should be kept in mind throughout the following contents of the texts.

Dear Reader, at this point in your deliberations, it would be apposite to turn to the end page 72 of this book to study the text that is headed:

HOW IT ALL STARTED

I recommend to the reader to study closely all the following Cameos. Indeed perhaps to read them several times to obtain and to absorb an overall understanding of the Cogent contained in this Work. Thus, most questions generated by the reader will be answered by virtue of this careful study.

PROOF VERSUS TRUTH

There is an apparent dichotomy in Proving (Feminine) the Truth (Masculine) in any matter under examination. Just consider the Telescope and the Binocular: The Truth enters through the front ends of these devices but without the internal placement of the splendidly constructed prisms, the proof does not appear to the eye at the back-end of these instruments - the viewing pictures are upside-down.

The Proof will manifest only via the inbuilt prisms within these devices. It is the same with any subject - there seems to be a world of difference between a theory and the practice of it; that is, the manifestation of the theory into concrete expressions and the costs involved in obtaining it in physical terms.

The prism and its function may be likened to the Formula required to bring a theory into practice, or the un-manifested to the manifested; the notion to its material reflection; the Truth to the Proven.

It is important to keep in mind that Feminine attributes are not necessarily all those of the female gender, and vice versa with Masculine attributes, these are not necessarily all those of the male gender - in absolute terms that is. Each male and each female have varying degrees of masculine and feminine qualities that help to determine their nature.

A spoken language that enjoys the richness of life's variants:

Neuter, Masculine and Feminine gender in its word meanings, nouns and adjectives, and which recognises these subtle divisions in all things, reveals a sensitive and a creative people.

These are people who embrace all aspects of life, both in their Masculine and in their Feminine form. That was almost certainly the case when the foundations of a given language were being developed for general usage.

As with most developed languages of the world, English did have word division in gender. This especial practice in Old English was in evidence before the 13th century A.D.

Neuter given to our language, was perhaps or perhaps not, a clever invention by The Powers That Be over an approximate 350 year period (800 A.D. to 1150 A.D.) probably to simplify the language, nay, free it from certain complications as they saw it, and establish a kind of equality and an equal value in the gravity of words for the day to day vocabulary.

It is probable that our Legal System developing within those Middle-Ages, led to a more simplified language usage to give The Laws of the Land, a practical and a comprehensible Stamp. This would enable all classes of people to understand them. An additional reason may have been the coming together and mix of different peoples from different lands, in England, at that particular epoch, but see **Page 70 so important!**

It is curious also, this change to gender neutrality arguably coincides, more or less, with the line of the first Saxon Kings: Egbert of Wessex being the first in-line.

He is acknowledged by scholars, to be the first of the English Saxon Kings circa 800 A.D., ending with the last of the Saxon Kings: Edmund II circa 1016 A.D. - his heirs completing the neuter to the English language, consciously or unconsciously.

The gradual payment or consequences for this fundamental change from gender usage to neuter in our language, became apparent as the centuries followed, and not immediately within the time period the sterilisation to gender in our word values took place.

The polemics involved with the gender changes to our language during that 350 year epoch, may have led ultimately to the degrading in the perception of subtle differences in the meaning and in the weight and in the power of words; particularly nouns and adjectives.

The gradual payment made and exacted, by nature, may have insidiously vulgarised even brutalised us all in varying degrees as a people, and especially so, the male gender of our English Speaking Nations.

We have gradually become de-sensitised to the exquisite division and separateness, but complementation of all things both temporal (Feminine) and ethereal (Masculine), within and around us.

For instance; the noun 'table' is usually feminine - being solid in material, and the noun 'curtain' is usually masculine - being less solid and more towards the diaphanous.

There are many reasons for this de-refining; partly because we have become an almost Godless society as very little is sacred anymore, and 'anything goes', and also partly because our language does not lure us to perceive subtle differences in the deeper meaning of words in their possible Masculine and in their Feminine form.

Of course there have to be many other reasons as well for this decline in our sensibilities in this matter.

The absence of gender duality in our language may have contributed to our being unable to see the natural division, and the relatedness in all things - a reason why we think of things in mono and not in stereo; bias in one direction and not the other direction; the other point of view that is always there and complementary. The other viewpoint is always inconvenient, a nuisance that should disappear.

This notion may also help to explain to some extent our sometimes boorish, coarse, even harsh attitudes and a sense of disrespect to and for others, especially in life's subtleties and, with the opposite sex, whether in abstraction (thought), or whether in material reflection (deeds). Cultivation and refinement is wanting - compared perhaps, with our European cousins. They may have a better attitude in these matters, but then, most other languages retain masculine and feminine gender in their nouns and adjectives.

The mode of thinking of any particular group, tribe or nation, will vary as regards to their language division between the male (*yang*) and the female (*yin*) in gender; that is, in their value to word meanings (nouns and adjectives). Word meanings in all that is structural and evident (*yin/feminine*), and in all that is ethereal and subtle (*yang/masculine*). See below:

Depending on the way of thinking of an individual, tribe or a nation, this representation of gender may be reversed.

For instance: that 'Form/Yin' may equate to Masculine and that 'Force/Yang' may equate to Feminine - the very opposite to the meaning of the way gender is expressed within the contents of this Book.

This may explain the way of thinking behind the *yang/yin* philosophy as applied in Macrobiotic Lore.

The founder of Macrobiotics (as such) the late George Ohsawa, explained much that appears contrary to the Chinese theory of *yin/yang*. Ohsawa taught *yin/yang* theory in reverse, changing its significance in practice - just another point of view of the same basic philosophy. Indeed it is not a mistake to think that the more gossamer a thing is, the more feminine it is, and the more solid a thing is, the more masculine it is.

However, taking what has been written about Heaven and Earth in the earlier pages of this Book, and to keep it all in simple terms: Heaven is given to Yang Masculine, and Earth is given to Yin Feminine and as written earlier: the ethereal energy of Heaven/Yang is centrifugal in nature and the temporal energy of Earth/Yin is centripetal in nature.

Heaven by compulsion attracts Earth, and Earth by compulsion attracts Heaven. Heavenly Yang energy being rarefied and by nature centrifugal, must DESCEND to realise itself materially and Yin energy being Earthly and by nature centripetal must ASCEND to realise and redeem itself by taking-on the Heavenly cloak of refinement and redemption - a perfect but beautiful arrangement that underscores all of creation. See Forward at the beginning of this Book.

It is likely that any confusion, if there is any, may be explained very simply by proffering the example of the function of the good old reliable Magnet. It is not sufficiently realised even by those 'in the know' that for a Magnetic Arm within a Compass to point to the North Pole, it [the magnetic arm] has to orientate with its South-end to do so. The Universal Law of Attraction of opposites is operative and unyielding: Yin attracts Yang; Male to Female etc., etc., Of the magnet - take two of them, place one negative end to the other magnet's positive end, and they can hardly be pulled apart.

Such is this powerful compulsion already referred-to.

The contrariness of male/female value as mentioned above with macrobiotic lore, may not matter too much and this difficult aspect is explained later in this Tome; what really matters is the sensitive perception of a Male/Yang and of a Female/Yin division that indicates a light-filled understanding by us that cannot always be reasoned or explained - it is a respect for, and a sensitivity to, and an awareness of The miracle of life in all its glorious multiplicity by virtue of this gender division.

NOTE: The gender division: male/female; positive/negative; force/form; sun/moon; yang/ yin; light/dark; hot/cold; abstract/concrete; left-side and right-side brain; is present in all that is seen and felt before our eyes and also that which cannot been seen and cannot be felt before our eyes. Further: those things initially hidden and intangible, in time, make themselves known by manifesting physically, emotionally and mentally, thus becoming objects and subjects. In common parlance: 'What goes around, comes around'.

IN ADDITION: Established physical, emotional and mental objects and subjects will inevitably, in time, disperse and disappear - their constituents breaking-up, becoming nebulous and thus returning to ethereal Heaven to begin another Cycle.

Empires come and go; ideas come and go; relationships come and go. As it says in the (David) Bible: "As for man, his days are like grass; he flourisheth like the flower of the field; for the wind passeth over it, and it is gone, and its place knows it no more "!

HELIOCENTRIC VERSUS GEOCENTRIC

Referencing recent statements from the above texts: Scientists calculate mathematically and with their conditioned beliefs (we all have conditioned beliefs both as blessings and as curses) that planet Earth revolves around the Sun. From the heliocentric viewpoint this is correct. This fact is sustained by the observation of the heavenly bodies moving in a predictable way in relation to one another, as from outer space - our Solar System in particular.

However, when on the surface of Mother Earth (geocentric view) we observe the Sun actually revolving around us, i.e. around the Earth. This motion and relationship is also correct. Especially so, because this mode of operation not only determines many important and obvious cycles of seasons and various rhythms in nature, but also determines those cycles outside and inside our bodies and minds, and the bodies and minds of all creatures.

In addition there are the cycles of day and night, birth and death etc., etc., notwithstanding the influences of the Moon phases and Motion.

The statements above represent two points of view, both of which are correct. The first statement: heliocentric viewpoint applying mathematics, observation, space calibration and imagination is perceived of right-side brain (Transcendence, Abstractions, Ideas, Abstract Mathematics: Truth). The second statement:

The geocentric viewpoint which implies a never ending movement, and has an 'energetic' but powerful affect assisting the cycles of nature and more (many aspects perhaps insidious) is perceived of left-side brain (Actually Seeing What Is, Material Proof).

The left-side brain functions are Feminine (formation; Proof and actuality), the right- side brain functions are Masculine (invisible forces; Truth as unseen but prime-moving).

Further: The left-side brain functions are: Seeing is believing; show me the evidence; hair-splitting; logic; and what you can see and touch is real; show me the Proof.

Right-side brain functions are: Believing is seeing; perceiving the whole and not giving precedence to the part; intuition; The Bigger Picture; visionariness; enlightenment; Truth. Knowing that there is involved a cosmic picture and a purpose.

To take this even further, if people look around them, they will see that the Earth is really flat - a few bumps here and there, but the land on which they live is basically flat, and that is all that matters for them as regards living a life that is rich and full or not as the case may be - it is good enough; lives are got-on with.

I think this could well be the motive behind the founding of The Flat Earth Society. The argument above I believe is quite legitimate. We only have to look around us to see with our own eyes that the Earth is flat. This viewpoint is a Feminine one because: 'what you see is what you get' and perfectly evident.

The masculine viewpoint is also correct, in that from a high vertical observation point, looking across and downwards, the Earth appears as spherical, and confirmed so, from the outer-space vista, and also of course by mathematical calculation. Confirmation of the spherical nature of the Earth might only be observable via the Heavens (Masculine).

In Church you remove your hat, and in the Synagogue you keep your hat on. The first viewpoint is Masculine, and the second viewpoint is Feminine - both correct. The Church exposes us to the light and the radiance within it (exposed head), and of the Synagogue, congregants wish only to hide themselves from the ethereal energies and radiance within it (covered head) - a kind of reverential but fearful attitude towards God, based-on traditional constraints and the mores of that people.

Judaism may be considered as Feminine in the terms as outlined in the texts above, because this religion adheres to the letter of the law/lore and the stability that its Tradition exhibits and demands.

Christianity on the other hand may be considered as Masculine because the contents of The New Testament are meant to be practiced with wider vision, spontaneity, revelation and openness, and the adaptation to each Age - meant to be?!?!

MALE & FEMALE ATTRACTION

Consider now Male and Female attraction. Let us look at the Female characteristics: Earth/Material-Formulation/Nurturing/Stabilising; she invites the attributes of the opposite and complementary Male to invade and often to control her. The reverse is also true - Male to Female.

Also, and this is the point: as Female is of the Earth and of the mundane and of the practical, (Earth attracts Heaven - Heaven on Earth) her interior aspirations are naturally lofty therefore, and she looks heavenwards for purpose of, and in life, and for, her redemption.

One of the reasons women are more refined and cultivated compared to the Male gender, is because they, the women perceive a higher need and purpose for the existence of Mankind and they do their best also to help cultivate the Male gender of the species to their betterment. SEE PAGE 71.

In a large percentage of cases with us Males, with some exceptions, we would be happy living inside caves as troglodytes, but for the Female aspirations of the women-folk, as well as for the dictates of the Feminine side of our own inner nature as men-folk.

Confidentially, there are many humans around us who consider it a badge of honour to behave and to look like the troglodytes wherever they may be!

I am reminded at this juncture of a little story told to me some fifty years ago, of a 25 year old young man reaching a dramatic 'cross roads' in his life, and his confusion as to which path he should choose to make something of his present but difficult incarnation.

He was fortunate enough to gain an audience with a celebrated and highly respected lady Guru from India visiting London at the time. She suggested to him in plain terms, when he spoke to her about himself and his life's-dilemma, to do four things before anything else: "One - get a haircut. Two - have a shave. Three - take a bath. Four - find a job, any job!".

Thomas Moore (1779-1852): "Disguise our bondage as we will......'tis woman, woman, rules us still".

The Male (Heaven/Force/Creation) by the law of attraction, needs to realise himself by absorbing the attributes of the mundane earthly world - these attributes are Female in origin (Heaven attracts Earth - Earth in Heaven). This may explain why un-redeemed man is predictably coarse and quite often obtuse and he tends to engage in those things that are base.

In time with his life experience, hopefully he becomes tame and even civilised once he has enjoyed the ruder and cruder aspects of what mundane life had and has to offer. Opposites are pulled to each other and we become similar to our opposites as the years pass!

Women have their strength within but are weaker without.

They, the womenfolk may create life by this arrangement - great interior strength is essential for the rigours of child bearing. Men have their strength and power exteriorly and are weaker within - the inside. Women are heavenly and softer on the outside, but earthly, strong and rigorous and therefore more stable interiorly. Men are earthy and rigorous on their outsides and heavenly, softer and vulnerable interiorly - one of the reasons why the male gender suffer more child mortality compared to the female.

The interior heavenly nature in the male gender should be evident more potently as time moves-on when in maturity, and so he becomes more civilised with this ageing process and even altruistic. He may even engage himself to the spiritual path to return to the Heavens, so to speak. The Earthliness of men's exterior frame is very useful of course, for the heavy duties life imposes on him. Altogether, this is a miraculous composition of mankind.

Dame Rebecca West (1892-1983): "There is of course, no reason for the existence of the male sex except that sometimes one needs help with moving the piano"

It is the awareness of the weaker interior the male gender suffers that the Ancients generated the need to devise the great disciplines of Hatha Yoga; Tai Chi and Chi Quong.

It was realised that Man as he is, even born with a constitution to be envied could still suffer the "slings and arrows of outrageous fortune health-wise" enough to cause him to stumble following several hammer-blows that life enjoys dishing-out.

These great disciplines were consciously created to strengthen and harden the interior body. Thus, the outer body may look-after itself. He may, therefore be able to concentrate more on his life's aims instead of enduring the distraction of having to give precious time worry and anguish to his health.

TO ADD EXTRA THOUGHTS AND FURTHER DEFINITION TO THE TEXTS ABOVE WITH SOME REITERATION:

Why and how may a woman, generally more civilised, physically more refined, be attracted to a man who is generally less cultivated, physically less refined and even brutish in comparison?

Is it because her task, as she is compelled by her inner being to do, to help refine him, and return him whole-some back to whence he came: Earth to be reflected in Heaven? Readers, please remember that opposites contain the inherent need/compulsion to bind together.

Woman aspires to bring Heaven to Earth as the true and higher purpose for her instinctual needs - she is of Earth in make-up and that attracts all Heavenly things.

Man aspires to make Earth manifest in Heaven as his true and higher purpose - he is of Heaven deep within and that compels/attracts him to Earthly things - initially!

Perhaps the more primitive the man, the more she feels she has a real purpose in refining him in his ways and his attitudes and thus assisting him in his life cultivation and perhaps, his final redemption. Hence, the attraction she has for him, on a physical, emotional and intellectual level. Though a friend of the wife of the author of this Book says:

"A glimpse of hell in the experiencing of a relationship with the opposite sex, is sufficient to make her aspire to the more elevated life, such as may be found within the Nunnery; some men are more hellish than others".......!

Perhaps the more cultivated and refined the woman, then the men feel the need to align and entrain with this attribute within her, in this way, to assist their own redemption. Or is it within this need to debase her and to side-track her, thus enabling her to grow in real strength when challenged in this way. (Women seem to possess greater endurance compared to menfolk).

From this, we may ascertain that there exists a very important argument in favour of the Entropic process in and on levels of existence, whether the victims are male or female. That is: The destructive forces of disorder in and of life, engendering chaos and resistance [Entropy] against the forces of creation and construction, thereby making creation and construction true and strong by virtue of that very challenge; makes for essential health and potency.

As P.D. Ouspensky said (paraphrased): "If life were perfect and unchallenged, then mankind would have to invent obstacles to maintain its (life) strength and vigour".

In individual lives this is also true, in that often the harder the life, the more success enjoyed materially, and spiritually in time. This is one of the reasons why foreigners, in the round, in their new country of residence may have no choice, but to work twice as hard as a does the individual from the indigenous population.

There is an argument arising from this as to how destructive a 'Nanny-State' will ultimately be, because of the weakening of its people and cushioning them against the normal vicissitudes that life will always produce whether good or ill.

This argument may extend to the absurd and the extreme, some might say, wholesale vaccinating of our children against childhood diseases, when childhood illnesses are there given by nature to 'kick-start' their Immune Systems for their future betterment, thereby standing them in good stead for the rest of their lives.

Confucius (c.550-c.478BC): "Our greatest glory is not, in never falling, but in rising every time we fall".

AS AN ASIDE AND FOR CONSIDERATION

The great religions of the world seemed to be jealously guarded, run and administered by the men-folk.

In my opinion, this is because God, or the Supreme Intelligence behind, beneath, within, without, and all around and the origin and architect of all creation, in His, or Its wisdom was able to witness in His, or Its creatures and especially so man, a wily and a corruptible mind and heart capable of conjuring-up and carrying-out terrible crimes and if not these, dreadful misdemeanours (Fallen Angels).

He or [It] imposed the great disciplines (religions) onto the men-folk to rein-in their minds and their hearts to enable some kind of order, ordinance, and civility as well as the notion of a higher purpose - meanwhile, we men-folk are 'lording it over' and think we are 'running the show', when in fact religious laws are there for our own good, imposed on us, because we have proven to be much of the time uncontrollable and/or guilty because we generate guile from deep within.

Bertolt Brecht (German dramatist 1898-1956): The wickedness of the world is so great that you have to run your legs off so you don't get them stolen from you. (The Threepenny Opera 1928).

As an aside: Brecht was a most curious and interesting man, having to leave Hitler's Germany for the United States because of his Avant-garde creative works. He always ensured he would wear a 2-day stubble on his lower face by shaving meticulously to achieve this effect. Thus the late singer and song writer George Michael with his 2-day designer stubble, had been 'pipped at the post' by as much as forty years.

To continue from the texts above: The women-folk, on the contrary do not need this religious control, or need it less so, as they are already there, so to speak, they are already filled with more grace and common-sense, and a higher purpose (Risen Angels) than menfolk - or were???

In this epoch 2000 A.D., plus, women in the round are trying to think, act and behave like the menfolk - consciously or subconsciously.

This may mean that there are strident women in the world now, who need to be redeemed as do most of us menfolk - some would argue, now the world is upside-down.

Further, as regards these statements above, women are forgetting their fundamental role in life and in society. A stupid man is sort of acceptable, but a stupid woman is not!

If women have forgotten their essential roles, then the male gender will certainly not know their roles either, as it is women generally who maintain the traditions and the stability of the family as well as the necessary teaching of civilised manners, etiquette and good- sense to keep society coherent.

Feed into your browser:

http://www.bandorians.co.uk/Gender%20Shock%202.mp3

A SONG OF LAMENT: GENDER JOLT

Why do some girls in this stressed Age

Just want to be, like us: The Crazed!

These girls have lost

their sweet gentility

and so endangered

their true humility

Because they are led, by rude modernity.

Why should a woman

want to be like as a man?

What is so splendid

about our clan?

To copy, to compete, why do they want to beat

us men into defeat!

Something has gone, so terribly wrong:

By them entering this mad worldly throng.

Copyright: Alexander Barrie

ALLOPATHIC MEDICINE

Another example similar to the Astronomical one, argued earlier within this book, is to look to the laboratories of Medicine. Experimentation is made with specific substances in finding a 'cure' for a given ailment.

This experimentation may take years to complete to enable a particular drug to be proven relatively safe for human consumption. Perhaps animals were used to gain the safety required to put this particular drug onto the market for the benefit of us humans!

Whether animals were employed or not in the experimentation, the science that underlies the experiment is usually sound and its methods may be replicated to enable this now reliable drug to be established and administered to combat the ailment for which it was originally designed. Mathematically and practically, and therefore indisputably, it appears that this compound substance deals with the symptoms of that disorder, but not necessarily a 'Cure' to it

What has **not** been measured or calibrated is the unseen or 'energetic' effect of the consumption of that drug either immediately or in time.

The bigger background picture, that cannot be measured with our existing instruments, usually has an unhinging effect on our various bodily physiological systems, if not on the more ethereal aspects of our human nature.

It would behove us to examine Dr. J. Oschman's works on 'Energy Medicine'. Sections of the contents of his books confirm in fact that there are devices nowadays that are sensitive enough to calibrate and register the unseen but energetic effects, adverse and otherwise to our physiology.

Retaining the theme of Truth (Male) and Proof (Female), the scientific confirmations, are deemed Feminine, and the unseen effects, in time, may be deemed Masculine, in that one gives an immediate practical result (Feminine/formation and practical detailed experimentation) and is perfectly legitimate, whilst the other gives a result not taken into consideration at the time and comes into being later:

An energetic disturbance and a perturbation that is detrimental to our overall physically engineered machine: The Body/Mind. (Masculine/immaterial/force and actual long-term experience in the field).

This last cameo indicates an extreme allopathic effect that may overwhelm, in time, the body's physiological systems. This circumstance may become the forerunner of the body's eventual derangement and subsequent illness because of the absence of not taking into consideration the possible long-term unhinging effects - detrimental effects with allopathic treatments that will probably manifest as ill-health in one form or another later-on in life. SEE PAGE 71.

GENDER VALUES IN NOUNS AND ADJECTIVES

How may a word that is a noun or an adjective, and which possesses a gender value evoke a way of thinking that enables mankind to appreciate two points of view/perspective, (Masculine/Feminine) according to the discussions within the texts above?

We continue to address a Ship (sea-going vessel) as SHE (Form). A remnant of the days we applied gender to our words. A SHIP given to the Feminine gender by most languages implies a structure; a covered place of safety and protection against the vagaries of the open ocean/sea. Though there is not a variation to this word indicating a masculine aspect (but there might be in other languages) - there is no need of it perhaps?

We could however, think in an abstract way as to what the Masculine aspect would be. For example: lateral thinking might prompt us into conceiving that there is a purpose to the voyage - business/trade yet to be carried-out and the safe delivery of goods and people to wherever; or even a voyage that is meant to be the execution of a Campaign of War.

This is the energetic side of things, the planning; thought and cogitation at first in the abstract - all a product of the Masculine Force. The Masculine Force being: conception and enterprise plus enthusiasm and vigour. Vigour required to operate a grand venture, to bring-in financial largesse primarily, and personal glory or vainglory secondarily!

The cogent point of this hypothesis is: that by returning nouns and adjectives to their gender value, which is not going to happen, an extra sensitivity would be exacted from us that would include a greater respect for the subtle differences and ideas life offers-up to us; ideas that on the face of it seem diametrically opposed (Male v. Female), yet with a little thoughtfulness allows us to go deeper gravitationally and to enjoy with understanding the two sides to the same coin, so to speak.

ADDITIONAL CAMEOS ON THE HYPOTHESES OFFERED

It is curious that, in the round, the Occidental World is dominated by music written in the Major Mode, and in particular: Popular Music. In the Oriental World, in the round, music composed is dominated by the Minor Mode.

In European Music Academies it is taught that the Minor Mode is born out of the Major Mode and that the Major Mode is Masculine whilst that of the Minor Mode is Feminine. (Not taught like this in the English Speaking World as it is embarrassing to the general ethos of the way we see gender, and is a bit too foreign for our liking!).

If the scale of the pure C Major Key (Whole and half tones): C—-D—-E-F—-G—-A—-B-C is examined it will be seen from the 6th note A and continued onwards to the next note of A one octave higher and retaining the same intervals of whole and semi-tones as in the C scale written above; when played on any instrument and especially in descending mode: A—-G—-F-E—-D—-C-B—-A, we derive the archetypal and pure Minor Key without sharps and flats, born out of the 6th note (rib?) of C Major.

All other Major Keys do not produce the same result from their 6th note, but do so only with sharps and flats. In Europe, Solfeggio is applied: Do—-Ray—-Me-Fa—-Sol—- La—-Si(T)-Do. As a musician myself, this nomenclature sounds much better to the ear, and some of whose names are from the Arabic.

It is interesting that the sound of the pure C Major Mode may be, according to some people, likened to the Sun in its brilliance, whilst from the 6th note A and in its descending mode may be likened to the Moon in its somber but magical reflection of light.

The first is Masculine - Solar (Sun), and the second is Feminine - Lunar (Moon). The First Sign of the Zodiac has a similar pattern, in that the First Zodiacal Sign Aries (Male) may be considered the most powerful (arguably) of the Zodiacal Signs (The Sun being exalted when in the Sign of Aries), and the 6th Zodiacal Sign of Virgo is (The Virgin) Female.

The Zodiacal Sign of Aries is considered in its nature as pure puissance and vigour, and the 6th Sign Virgo in its nature as pure, refined and cultivated physical material from and of: Earth.

The scale of C Major may be played ascending and descending without the need for sharps and flats, and the scale of A for the Minor Mode does so, but is more pure in sombre sound in the descending manner.

In addition and in numerological terms, the number 6 is given to the Planet Venus by many Traditions - She being the Goddess of Love and Harmony and visually and actually the archetype of exquisite feminine celestial grace and beauty rarely seen now in the Western World, but is almost commonplace in the Oriental World. The quality of this true Femininity is sufficient to engender from the Male species: speechlessness, wonder and awe - enough to bring him to his knees and automatically and instinctively behave with respect and dignity towards her. This now is almost unknown in our Western World, since in the mad race for women to do as we, the men do, they are unaware of their loss of grace and many of the exquisite feminine attributes.

In the present day ethos of women's freedom which is to do what they like willy-nilly in carrying-out men's work, thinking as men do and behaving as men do, they will suffer a terrible dearth of grace and femininity and a nation of Spinsters will result in addition to other hideous abnormalities - they may become brutalised in the competitive outside world with the madness of success and failure!

Indeed, the representation of the Archetypal Female ('...but where have these beautiful daughters of Venus gone, now that they, the daughters, are acting, thinking and behaving like us men-folk as mentioned above) may be embodied within The Music Minor Mode from the note A as it descends in scale. The descent, in a sense, is to Earth and has already been discussed.

The pure Major Key C may move both ways ascending and descending and still be pure and the same in sound both ways, indicating perhaps, Heaven's manifestations in two directions - The Omnipresence.

Each Musical Note traditionally has an attribute: The Note A is considered, amongst other things, The Note of Sadness and Pensiveness.

It is interesting that in an assembly of different religions of the world, some have at the beginning of their Religious Services a prayer that the menfolk repeat, and that goes something like: Thank you God for not making me a woman......and all the travail that that means...!

Generally, most people would agree that the Major Mode (Masculine) is lighter and sunnier and open in mood and expression.

The Minor Mode is heavier, earthier, thoughtful and **sensual** in mood and expression, and that may be a laudable definition for this Mode. However, music of sadness, it is true, may also be written in the Major Mode and also carry with it deep mournfulness.

It is natural to repeat a phrase in music. Indeed, instinct demands it. Not to repeat the first phrase or first movement feels musically amiss. Even if this repetition is slightly modified as commanded by the spirit in the writing of the composition - it is still an echo, a confirmation, an affirmation of the first phrase or first movement.

The initial phrase or movement is Masculine, and the echo, the repeated statement is Feminine. The Masculine part initiates and the Feminine part confirms and stabilises.

Great music applies both Major and Minor forms as well as Neuter in the way of the application of Whole Tones (Debussy); Discordance; Dodecaphonic Atonal (Schoenberg et al) and the Gypsy/Oriental Minor Mode.

ASTRONOMY V. ASTROLOGY

Astronomy may be deemed the Feminine aspect, and Astrology may be deemed the Masculine aspect of Cosmology. Astronomy has to do with measurement, calibration, mathematics, precision, weight, gravity, Space/Time Theory, origins and movement of heavenly bodies and more, and looks to Proof and what is.

It is all about mechanics, and therefore of the Feminine Aspect and the seeing of this reality as it is, with the great material bodies in Space, including our Mother Earth.

Astrology may be deemed Masculine and has to do with the effects of the movements of the heavenly bodies on and in life on Planet Earth. That is, the vicissitudes of individual lives and the destiny of nations and monarchs, etc., driven by the especial movements of the Planets and the significance of the Sun and the Moon in their various positions at any one time in the Heavens.

These are considered, certainly by the Ancients as Truth, and Prime-Moving - notwithstanding the planetary and star effects on the geophysics of the Earth and on vegetation and on animals.

Both aspects of Cosmology outlined above are equally perfect legitimate views.

Ptolemaic Astrology, (Greek Astronomer and Astrologer Claudius Ptolemy circa A.D. 100-178) which is the Astrology mostly deployed in America, Britain, Europe and the Near East uses as one of it tools: The Zodiac, but symbolically not actually as it is in the Heavens:

Beginning from the First Point of Aries (the First and the Prime Sign of the twelve Signs of The Zodiac), as happens at the first moment/point when it appears that the Sun crosses the (Celestial) Equator. This is when day and night are equal in length and this position is called: The Vernal Equinox (The Spring Ingress).

Astrological interpretation by this symbolism is deemed Masculine and therefore tends to be: notional and a tendency towards, and an inclination to, and prone to induce events and happenings for and in, human behaviour.

There are a number of religions and a number of secular nations in the world that begin their New Year from the First Point of Aries aforementioned (April 21st approximately of any one year).

Further and again:

This Vernal (Spring) Equinox represents the moment, or the point where the ecliptic (the earth's apparent pathway in its journey within the Solar System; but for us on Earth, it is the Sun that we observe in movement/action) dissects the circle of the (Celestial) Equator. This is also known as the first degree of the Tropical Zodiac and it begins at the First Degree of the Sign of Aries. This is the time of the Vernal (Spring) Equinox as already mentioned above.

From this First Point of Aries, all the other Zodiacal Signs follow in from their traditional order and each Sign is given a 30° arc. There are Twelve Zodiacal Signs. 12 x 30° = 360°. This completes the calibrated belt around the sphere (The Zodiac).

The Crossing Over or Passing Over, from the esoteric viewpoint, constitutes one of the meanings of the Judaic Passover.

In the Christian Tradition this Passing Over is celebrated at the period of the Crucifixion when in Remembrance. Remembrance, that is the institution of the Eucharist (Easter Time).

The Last Supper of Jesus Christ (*J(Y)esu ben J(Y)oseph*) was at the beginning of the Passover Festival Observance.

As has been stated: the time of the Vernal Equinox marks the first day of the New Year for many peoples' of the world, both religious and secular.

Importantly day and night are equal in length as darkness and lightness have the same time period.

Therefore, it may be stated that the male and the female gender in creation, are equal and the same in value at these time periods, including the Autumn Equinoctial phase of course.

These times of equality may be thought-of as Affirmations. Affirmations in this case meaning that neither one gender is superior nor inferior to the other.

In addition, they are made equal by the Winter (Female-*Yin*) merging into Summer via Spring, and by Summer (Male-*Yang*) merging into Winter via Autumn.

Traditionally, in Old Testament times, a holy teacher required 12 disciples - each to represent one of the 12 Signs of the Zodiac; the Zodiacal Signs embodying all possible departments of life on Earth. A Holy Man was considered 'A Son of God' in the Hebrew/ Cabalistic tradition.

THE CABBALA REVEALS:

Heaven's aspiration is to manifest itself in and on Earth in myriad ways. Thus, a miracle is beheld, because Heaven is manifested in Earth in this way. Further: His need, His desire, is to reveal Himself in and by all earthly means. It is like: His (Heaven/ Masculine) holding a mirror up to Himself (Earth/Feminine) that reflects His image and in this way an actual declaration is made of His physical Masculine attributes, but also, as in myriad ways, his Feminine Form as well.

The statement above alludes to the unification of opposites: An IDEA (Masculine) initially invisible, then expanding outwards with its centrifugal force employing its brilliant light, heat, sound and **Will** to do so, to enable: Eventual condensation into matter that is centripetal, with all the possible elements within this matter (Feminine), that science (an aspect of the workings of God's mind) may study, absorb, notate, enjoy but also: suffer!

In this way, we have the two sides to the same entity, so to speak, each side requiring the other to realise Creation in its fullness. Put another way: Explosive Potent Energy that is immediate, and its physical expression, that requires TIME (maybe billions of years) to appear into the FORMATIONS as we know them, including our own BEING.

Albert Einstein: "The only reason for time is so that everything does not happen at once"

Lie Zi, a Daoist philosopher who lived circa 300 B.C., said: " The purer and lighter [elements] tending upwards made Heaven; the grosser and heavier [elements], tending downwards, made Earth"

The Creationists and the Darwinists, typical of human behaviour, see themselves in opposition and not in harmony - harmony that the texts above attempt to convey: The Biblical Seven Days to construct Heaven &

Earth should be read as symbolical in that 1 Day is equivalent to 0.649 billion Years. Therefore 7 Days multiplied by 0.649 Billion Years equals 4.543 Billion Years - this number is the estimated age of the Earth. The plan in conception and then execution took 7 Days, but the final result in actual construction took 4 Billion Years plus - The thing is:

Who or What conceived, and then had that notion executed????????

It is rarely considered nowadays, because under the scientific ethos of the age in which we live, it is embarrassing to do so, that the main and true purpose of the 12 and true members of the Jury, were to arrive at a fair and just verdict within a Court of Law.

Established in the twelfth century, the Twelve Members of The Court Jury were there to represent The Twelve Basic Types of man and woman according to the Twelve Zodiacal Astrological Birth Signs.

Thereby, they, The Jury should arrive at a wholesome verdict at any given Trial. Each juror represents one twelfth of all the matters and manifestations of creation on Earth.

Of course it was not feasible to find twelve people all of whom represent individually the twelve Astrological Signs according to their birth date and times. No, what mattered and matters was/is the SYMBOLICAL effect this arrangement of The Twelve could engender.

The Twelve Zodiacal Signs may teach us many things. For instance: Six of the Signs are deemed Feminine and the remaining six are deemed Masculine. This is a universal representation of Male & Female equality, and their inextricable relationship; for the Signs Male & Female alternate and interweave with one another. These Twelve Signs also RULE everything that is manifest and everything that is un-manifest within our Solar System - all that is in Creation as we know it and as we do not know it.

Though nowadays things are changing, it is sad that we the male gender still dominate our female counterparts mistakenly thinking we are superior and especially so the further East we go in this world.

It is this stupid unthinking attitude that has brought-about and is bringing-about womankind to lose its celestial femininity and modesty (particularly in the West, as mentioned above) as it struggles to think, act and do in the world what we, the male gender, have done since the beginning of time.

Nowadays, it is not enough that womankind may create life - man cannot do this; he has to create, but that is to create something in the world in his memory, and in this way attempt to leave his permanent mark usually by the means of his career - she is doing that very thing now as well, as dictated by the strange ethos of this epoch, to do the things that men desire and even have to do. As a result she becomes less feminine, she loses that priceless attribute of Grace (that powerful quality that men truly adore and which makes them fall at the feet of this rare breed of women), she becomes too manly and this curse drives men away from her because they, the menfolk are too frightened and worse: confused. Confused such as to cause the menfolk difficulties in making overtures to them. I predict from now, as stated above, there will be generations of spinsters. Wars that killed-off the menfolk was the way of doing this in the 'old days' - but now this is the new way of the production of the unmarried.

Of course women do good work in the world often better than us menfolk, but let them be aware, because they are not aware, that as they do this madness in the world, as we menfolk do, they will mostly lose their wonderful and seductive quality of priceless womanhood.

Confidentially, such abnormal arrangements nowadays is spectacularly favourable to the cosmetic industry, because women somehow will know unconsciously what modernity has caused them to become and steeped-in, that is, in their new manliness, and they will therefore apply, and do cosmetics to attract the opposite sex as they become aware of their lack of charm - charm and innocence that forms the basis of attraction for men towards women.

The cosmic layout of Zodiacal Signs was meant, amongst other things, to represent and to assist the coming into being of equality between the sexes - each of us needing the other and complementing the other for: 'Completion'.

We the male gender have tended to operate by taking charge of the 12 departments of life (The Twelve Astrological Signs) when we should be doing so for six of them only. The other six Signs belong to and are within the realm of the female gender to manage.

There is some cross-over of course, but the dominance to six of the Signs with one particular gender is always there or should always be there.

As an aside, most of us have limited knowledge of Astrology per se. Our awareness of it is mostly from newspaper and magazine columns.

It is important that these Sun-Sign predictions and comments as presented should be understood as Fair-Ground and High-Street Shopping astrology. This bastardised form of the art does little to convey the seriousness of its science. Its science and its philosophy are boundless and these attributes are profound when it comes to their interpretations within the astrological construct.

Amongst the most notable names of geniuses of the past and especially so in conventional science are: Confucius; Aristotle; Plato; Dante; Shakespeare; Sir Francis Bacon; Goethe; Baron Napier (inventor of logarithms); Pythagoras; Hippocrates (Father of Occidental Medicine); Sir Isaac Newton; Copernicus; Galileo; John Flamsteed 1646-1719 First Astronomer Royal at the Royal Observatory Greenwich London; and more............

When introducing these Names for teaching and historical purposes, it has become undesirable to mention their fascination for the Art of Astrology and their actual practice of it. In the 'olden days' this cosmology was not divided - Astronomie was the name and spelling given to astronomy and astrology combined.

MEDICINE

In taking the arguments further as regards the energetic/rarefied unseen effect of a prescribed drug not normally taken into consideration by the orthodox establishment in Medical Practice, the polemics implicated in the struggle between Orthodox and Alternative Medicine is highlighted following the texts above (the reader should keep in mind the Proof/ Truth theme):

Last words of Alexander the Great just before he expired: "I am dying with the help of my physicians"

Orthodox Medicine, generally State sponsored, and particularly dominant in practice in Occidental countries may be deemed Feminine in character according to the arguments given within the previous texts.

The panoply of pathological Conditions that we humans suffer are studied scientifically in the laboratory to understand their nature and therefore also, to establish a countermeasure, usually through drugs and surgery to assist elimination of that ailment. Even so, Trauma is superbly dealt with by Orthodox Medicine, and of course it is perfectly legitimate and has its rightful place in the scheme of things.

Benjamin Franklin (1706-1790):

"He's the best physician that knows the worthlessness of most medicines". See page 51.

Alternative/Complementary Medicine, mostly originating from Oriental Lands, with a few exceptions, may be deemed Masculine in character according to the arguments within the previous texts. Trauma aside, the panoply of pathological Conditions we humans suffer are considered the results of our body/mind Systems being: 'out of energetic balance' but also because most of these Physiological Systems are overloaded with toxic substances. See below:

THE RELEVANCE OF THE ACID/ ALKALINE BALANCE OF THE FLUIDS WITHIN THE BODY:

Most of us eat more acid forming foods than alkaline forming foods - habit! This common mode of eating tends to engender excess acidity within the fluids of the body which includes the state of the blood of course. This imbalance is potentially detrimental to our health because it means an acidic build-up that may damage in time our bones, joints, ligaments, tendons, muscles and other tissues. Our physiological system of checks and balances within the body itself are put under great strain in neutralising excess acid build-up - the body neutralises excess acid inefficiently when overwhelmed with acidic producing foods.

The physiological intelligence within the body will push excess residues of these acids away from the vital organs, and what it cannot eject via bodily waste mechanisms, will deliver the remnants or residues of this waste to the bony joints; the ligaments especially and other related structures.

The malefic effects are as follows:

MESENTERY - this internal abdominal structure is weakened when it has absorbed toxic residues such as to cause it to sag and swell and because of this it tends to protrude (beer belly). Also the abnormal pulling forward of a balloon-like heavy belly may engender a lordosis of the lumbar spine weakening the lumbar spinal segments in that situation. In addition, this abnormality may have detrimental consequences to the other segments of the spine. Prolapsed visceral organs as with the intestines are also important factors to consider with the weakening of the abdominal cavity.

INTERVERTEBRAL DISCS (cartilage) - may physically contract and harden thus lessening mobility and flexibility of the segments of the spine leading to stiffness and pain and the horrible potential of the rupturing of an intervertebral disc.

LIGAMENTS - when these absorb acid residues, they may become weak, brittle and contracted and therefore they will lose their flexibility and so distortion of bony joints and subluxations is inevitable because these ligaments are attached to relevant bones.

In fact it means that this ligamental impairment must have a deleterious affect on all the bony joints of the whole spine and the sacroiliac joints of the pelvis especially.

MUSCLES - excess acid residues may be injurious to various muscle systems. Some muscles becoming too tight and stiff and others becoming too soft and flaccid. This places an extra strain on the bony joints of the whole anatomical frame and so dislocation of these junction points may occur - commonly the bony articulations of the pelvis and all weight-bearing joint-hinges suffer - hyper & hypo-mobility of a joint will cause abnormality of movement, if any, and so the whole skeletal frame may suffer.

OSTEOPOROSIS - acidity may leach-out mineral calcium from the body complex, and with the bones especially - we need to be aware of the serious consequences to the weakening strength of the bones when this occurs.

THE BONY SPINAL SEGMENTS (vertebrae) - it is not only the intervertebral disc that deteriorates as indicated above, but also the spinal segment itself is in detriment.

They, the vertebral segments, may shrink and harden, enough to lessen the size of the foramina (small openings) that are at the root of the spinal processes and through which pass the nerve fibres. In this way, groups of nerve fibres are constricted and cannot move (they require a small amount of movement back and forth) - thus, they the nerve fibres, are being abnormally compressed. Because of this compression, pain and problematic effects to all structures including the visceral organs may occur and so they become deficient in their functions because the electrical and biological impulses which these fibres conduct, will do so in an abnormal and in a limited way. The twelve cranial nerves, originating from the brain itself, may not escape this scenario of dysfunction either.

Avoiding the body-interior scenario as outlined above, it would be wise to lessen the intake of acid producing foods and to increase the consumption of alkaline producing foods such as with vegetables and certain grains though preferably organic in origin.

Log-onto: naturalhealthschool.com

ENVISAGE THE HUMAN SPINE
AS A METAL SPRING/COIL

Picture the human spine as a strong flexible metal spring that may be bent virtually in all directions (from end to end it may move up and down as well as side to side) and capable of contraction, expansion and torsion clockwise and anti-clockwise. The spine's intervertebral discs endow it with this capability of springiness. Its tensile strength exists because of the three specialised ligaments threading through and holding the vertebrae and the intervertebral discs against one another in their correct positions.

It is in the nature of this construct to enjoy safe osteopathic adjustments when segments have marginally become misaligned and corrective procedures administered.

By electing to choose a useful form of exercise or discipline (see below), which bends and contorts this magnificent tensile spring: the spine, you are loosening acid residues and any sediment trapped, stuck and lodged within the structures of the vertebral joints of your spine.

Thus, you are assisting it to maintain its health by keeping it clean and free of inflexibility. There is a commensurate increase in blood flow and therefore nourishment both to the cartilaginous discs and the segments of the spine.

ESSENTIAL GUIDE NOTES TO ASSIST ALIGNMENT OF PELVIS AND SPINE TO REDUCE AND EVEN ELIMINATE BACK-PAIN AND THEREFORE ALL OTHER MUSCULOSKELETAL ACHES & PAINS

The Pelvic Corrector Device* when used to re-adjust the pelvis and spine is the most perfect way of giving maintenance to the spine thereby helping it return back to its original pristine state.

*www.alexaligntherapies.com www.alignedwellnessacademy.com

In addition to possible 'workouts' as alluded-to above, it may be understood now why any kind of bodywork, massage particularly on and over the spine, will be beneficial as they help to keep it, the spine supple and healthy. In the author's opinion, Shiatsu and related therapies are probably the most powerful and best form of bodywork that may be enjoyed and even revered !

Manual 'bodywork' may assist detoxification of the physiological body, but a discomforting re-action could occur especially the following day.

Undertaking a discipline such as with Hatha Yoga (Hat-Yog), Tai Chi, Chi Kung, means that you have cleansed your body sufficiently to enjoy, for example Shiatsu treatments as mentioned above without the discombobulating discomforting re-action that sometimes happens with the first and second treatments. Put another way: subsequent fall- out after the 'nuclear explosion' of a treatment, should help avoid a difficult re-action.

Though The Alexander Technique (no relation to the author or relationship to Pelvic Correction) and Pilates are excellent disciplines, only those ancient practices mentioned above strengthen the interior body, that is: the visceral organs. Workouts at gymnasiums (Gyms) are alright, but these only strengthen the outer body - the interior body remains weak. If any of the ancient disciplines are engaged and which strengthen the interior body, the outer body is made strong an healthy spontaneously.

SMOKING

It has been proven by research and observation that smoking, which includes the smoking of narcotics, engenders the fine network of blood vessels within the vertebral segments of the spine to contract in size. This is very undesirable, because the way to keep intervertebral discs healthy and with their inherent springiness is for them to take their nourishment from their adjacent vertebral segments. The narrowing of these fine blood vessels, restricting blood flow tends to disable the process of the normal blood supply, so the vertebral segments suffer health-wise and in turn, so do the intervertebral discs and subsequently, the whole spine is on a trajectory to deteriorate in its health and therefore in its proper function.

When we humans stand erect, compression of the intervertebral discs takes place and when we humans lie-down, our intervertebral discs swell somewhat because the cartilaginous discs are receiving nourishment from their adjacent spinal segments (vertebrae).

Therefore, in addition to a regular night's sleep, it is recommended for him/her to enjoy a 'siesta' sometime during the day. The health of the spine should improve simply because it is horizontal at rest - the vertical pressure is temporarily removed as the cartilaginous discs are re-invigorated.

Hanging upside-down, using an inversion machine should now be seen as beneficial as well. This dangling stretch tends to opens-up the whole of the spinal construct.

Also, undertaking the so-called 'chin-up' that is: dangling your body, right way up, by using your hands to hold firmly a support bar of sorts will have a similar favourable effect also.

THE HEALTH OF THE COLON IS INVOLVED IN MAINTAINING A STABLE PELVIS - THE PELVIS READILY DISLOCATES AND IS THE SOURCE OF 98% OF BACK-PAIN.

It is more than likely that a large percentage of us suffer with the interior fungal infection of different sorts of Candida. The body's immune system cannot always cope with these parasitic entities, indeed, Candida might be thought of as a pestilential plague of sorts.

It affects us, mentally, emotionally and physically in a destructive way.

In maintaining a modicum of health in life, for which we have to fight and to struggle to do, because it lessens the joy of living it, it is essential to exercise the body, thus to acquire a stabilising System of sorts to render the Mind peaceful and to keep the Emotions balanced. Even so, there are a few of us strange Beings, who wallow in all kinds of suffering to be savoured - 'it takes all sorts' as it is said!

The ill-affects of Candida may well be the reason behind certain inconvenient food allergies some of us experience. We may include in this an adverse re-action to pollen as well. There may also be a vaccination element, amongst other things, giving rise to the rejection of certain food stuffs. That is, vaccination forced on us in our childhood. (One day in the not too distant future, it will be discovered that the wholesale vaccinations given to us all, child and adult, was similar to giving us a death sentence!).

Candida's greatest felon is injury to the Colon - its main place of residence. Possessing a 'sweet tooth' is a detriment which ideally should be addressed very seriously - it compels us to consume sweets, chocolate, cakes, ice cream and various fruits. (Remember the advice above on acid/

alkaline). The health and strength of the Colon most definitely has a profound effect on the stability of the bony pelvis, and the spine generally.

Probably the most natural antidote to candida is the proper use of formidable garlic (the wonder vegetable but it should be **organic**). Best consumed cooked, as raw garlic may engender inconvenient diarrhoea. Garlic pearls (pills) are acceptable, but the actual raw clove is best but cooked. Honey mixed with prepared raw garlic cloves may be eaten together without having to cook the garlic itself.

BACK-POCKET SCIATICA & COLD WINDY WEATHER

Placing a wallet or such like into your back pocket should be avoided, because as you sit, the horizontality of the pelvis may be seriously compromised. Also this forced posture may place abnormal pressure onto the piriformis muscle at the ball and socket joint of the hip, thus contributing to pelvic misalignment. (Ole Larsen - Headache And Back-pain - Let It Go).

It is recommended that you maintain a covered abdomen (belly) and lower back lumbar region at all times. The kidneys loath coldness and chill. Their efficient functioning is vital for healthy bones and maintenance of strength and the Will to do - they require warmth to keep them healthy.

According to Chinese Medicine Lore, they [the kidneys] hold our money in the bank energy-wise; in simple terms they are our batteries and supply power to the rest of the visceral organs of our bodies and more. Keep your belly (Hara) and your lower back warm at all times.

Do not follow ridiculous and stupid fashion that tends to produce garments that expose our most precious parts, abdomen and lumbar, to all and sundry including to cold, windy and wet weather.

Lifting any object, weighty or otherwise, should be performed without a twisting motion - always be square-on to the object you lift, and you may avoid your back giving- way engendering pain and the depressing thought that you have suddenly aged 20 years.

Actually, there is no food substance that has an absolute value acid/alkaline-wise. Some people need more acid producing foods than alkaline producing foods according to their body-type. Log-on

45

to: naturalhealthschool.com for the science and more behind the theory and food categories of acid and alkaline.

Further: There are, curiously, some natural acidic plant based foods that actually alkalise the body and are recommended for consumption, and they are: Lemon; tomato; orange; pineapple; and cayenne pepper. Once their mineral content of these foods is absorbed physiologically, they alkalise the body fluids.

To resume the matters of Medicine: *Chi or Qi or Prana* are the oriental names that possess special meaning as regards to the 'life force' in all living things - this must include inanimate objects as well, but also places that have atmosphere such as the insides of prisons and the interiors of churches.

Be taken blindfolded into a building and you will know which one is church-like and which one is prison-like and in this way a depression to the soul, or the opposite indeed. Then you will begin to understand the different qualities of *Chi*.

Our language lacks the word required to express the true meaning of what it is to maintain a healthy lifestyle to enable us to endure its lease of time whilst living this earthly life - our word 'longevity' may be applied but it does not explain sufficiently the special nuances.

Trauma aside, doctors of medicine would see there role slightly differently if they read via a good lexicon the true definition of the word: Physician. It carries the meaning of: One who is skilled in the Art of Healing!

The expertise and the theories underscoring Alternative Medicine are perfectly warranted, being perceived as the other usually unseen side of the matter. Many consider the implementation of A.M. in all its myriad forms to be the only Medicine that deals with the Truth regarding Pathology - because it recognises the Lifestyle of the patient having profound effects on his/her wellbeing and consequently the ailments that may or may not follow-on.

To convey the deeper, meaningful expression that is *Chi:* Initially its meaning has to be grasped mentally after which it is to be felt, and in this way comprehended in all its subtleties.

Only in recent years is Science recognising the presence everywhere of this force that has many guises. It is not quite material and it is not quite ethereal, yet it is both in its pure form or formlessness?

Imagine a substance that is both a combination of matter and energy, and that carries with it a power that is both of Earth and of Heaven and how potent that blend would be. It is this that is *Chi*.

Electricity and magnetism are forms of *Chi* and the subtle way homeopathic remedies work seem very good examples of the *Chi* of the remedy neutralising the *Chi* of the ailment.

There are different forms and different mixes of *Chi* as already touched-upon. These combinations all do specialised work.

Traditional Chinese Medicine (pre-1949) in its application and its philosophy defines in an inspired and in an elegant way the different purposes of this treasure that gives life and maintenance to the body/mind/spirit.

Rupert Sheldrake's Morphic Resonance is *Chi* of a kind (say that of a tree) that has the capacity to communicate within its own breed over time and space, but also with other life-forms.

Further, when meeting or greeting a family member or friend or acquaintance or stranger, usually we perceive their general physical, mental and emotional state; not only from their body language and facial expression but by the quality of vigour and ether they are exuding - this is a form of *Chi* also.

We may be fortunate enough to experience *chi* in the priceless form of '*dynamism*' when in excellent health, and we may feel it in a moment of ecstasy. It may be increased with positive thinking as well as with positive feelings, but it is also increased with the practices of the ancient disciplines that came into being long ago as mentioned earlier in this Book precisely to prolong and to maintain life.

Referring back to our splendid gender divide, the denser and more concentrated Chi is and therefore centripetal in nature, the more Yin or Feminine it is - the more rarefied and fine Chi is and therefore centrifugal in nature, the more Yang or Masculine it is.

BACK-PAIN

"Aunt Agatha's demeanour now was rather like that of one who, picking daisies at the railway, has just caught the down express in the small of the back"

(The Inimitable Jeeves 1923. By permission of A.P.Watt Ltd., on behalf of the Woodhouse Estate)

In practice there are a number of medical skills that deal successfully and unsuccessfully with this musculoskeletal corrosive and commonplace Condition.

Just a few of these medical approaches to back-pain have certain attributes in common; and if they are science based, then they do not work terribly well; being mostly drug and/or surgery based to assist amelioration of this overwhelming problem of which mankind suffers.

These ways of dealing with backache are science and logic based applying modern technology which is limited in its medical understanding as it looks to the dysfunction directly without standing back to perceive the whole picture - the man, the woman as they actually are as regards to their lifestyle and general habits, way of thinking plus a multitude of other factors does not usually enter the diagnostic picture. This Reductionist approach is the Feminine gender way, but still, of course, has value in diagnosis as it examines in concentrated detail what is.

Other alternative ways of viewing this accursed problem of back-pain and ache is the way that is more intuitive and wider in view, for the disorder presented; which is to stand- back and allow an insightful response from the physician. A response that should help reveal the underlying reason for the causes of the skeletal frame to dislocate at various junction points. Needless to say this is the Masculine gender viewpoint and is wider in its application..

Thus, it is well to stabilise the pelvis, being The foundation of the skeletal frame, the pelvis is always culpable with its bony dislocations. Once the pelvis is stabilised, life should become sweeter and under some control health-wise, and so this pestilential syndrome of back and all the attendant musculoskeletal-skeletal aches and pains may be lessened and/or eliminated. Leg length discrepancy is 98% of the time a product of pelvic dislocation.

IMPORTANT ADDITIONAL INFORMATION ON: PELVIC ALIGNMENT

Until the pelvis is stabilised, and the efforts of the sufferer must be called upon to assist in the healing process, then back-pain and other musculoskeletal aches and pains will always be experienced throughout the life of its carrier i.e. You and Me!

The back-pain Condition is at the top of the list of human pathologies along with attendant aching joints: wrist, elbow, shoulder, neck, hips, knees, ankles and feet. Not to forget the scourges of lumbago and sciatica and frozen shoulder; golf and tennis elbow.

Headache and digestive disorders, amongst other ailments, are pathologies very much tied-up with non-alignment of the skeletal frame and the pelvis especially.

Visceral organs pulled out of place are much vexed (they have their own intelligence), and because of this, obstructions to their biological and electrical conduction, inducing inefficient physiological processes, are the root causes of so much of these disharmonious and commonplace occurrences in our personal life psychologically as well as diseases to the soma.

There exist special techniques to bring to the pelvis the stability it needs and therefore also to the spine in general: www. alexaligntherapies.com

Of course there are many instances when conventional drugs and/or surgery are necessary to administer, and also the belief system within a given epoch of a particular Country East or West will or may determine conventional or traditional treatments serving a particular disorder. See below:

HOMEOPATHY & MEDICAL SCIENCE:

In recent years there have been science based tests to ascertain the validity of Homeopathic Medicine's claims. In my own experience the efficacy of this type of medicine is only as good as the homeopath's experience and knowledge and subsequent administration. Given the correct remedy or remedies prescribed, the therapeutic results are usually spectacular.

Testing this type of medicine, knowing that the theory that underlies it, is complicated, makes it almost impossible to create a test to prove its efficacy. Tests that were undertaken in the recent past proved damning in their results causing confusion amongst those who have been and are successfully treated homeopathically and doubt in the minds of those who were considering such a form of medicine to be of help in reducing the effect of, or even eliminating their ailments.

It has already been written earlier in this Book that science based medicine is a Feminine aspect (according to the object of this book) and so requires rigorous procedures to validate the efficacy of medicines and certain medical procedures for administration but not necessarily for curing the disease but only in assisting elimination of its particular symptoms (allopathic medicine).

Different procedures are necessary when attempting to validate homeopathy because we are dealing with rarified energy (*Chi*). A different and a more sensitive form of test is required in vindicating the deployment of this type of therapeutic treatment.

Homeopathic remedies work energetically/ethereally (a Masculine aspect) to help to push and pull the physiological system back into better balance thereby eliminating and/or reducing the ailment in question.

Homeopathic remedies operate by introducing a challenge into the body-soma in the form of a substance, but this substance contains within it a particular characteristic form of rarefied *Chi*, the essence of which is used to displace an existing ailment the body or part of the body suffers.

The nature and the specific energies of this existing ailment are confronted with the same kind of essence that would give similar unpleasant symptoms as does the ailment in question, and this essence is introduced into the body-soma homeopathically.

Thus both these similar energies confront each other and push each other out of the body- system. That is: **fighting like with like.**

As mentioned in the early texts about the conventional magnet: of two separate magnets, touch both positive or both negative ends together and the magnets repel each other. The principle is the same homeopathically when the rarefied essence of a given substance is pitted against an existing condition that has the same or similar rarefied pith that causes unpleasant symptoms, then that ailment is displaced, even eliminated - though this process may require several attempts, because certain medical Conditions are very stubborn to expunge.

Apart from choosing the right remedy for a given ailment, the trick is also to ascertain the correct potency of the remedy to be given. Such may have to be empirical in that the lower potencies leading up to the higher potencies may have to be applied to obtain the expected therapeutic effect. The more chronic a Condition, the more complicated the administration usually and the more time it will take to dislodge that Disorder.

Regarding the dislodgement or displacement of a Condition and the actions of repulsing magnets; when introducing into the body the perfect remedy with the perfect potency that may be of very high strength (high strength means virtually no trace of the essence of that substance) it is as though the essence of the disorder already within the body, takes fright and makes a quick exit. Why? Because in common parlance: you cannot have two engine drivers working one steam-engine!?!?

It is the ethereal or rarefied essence mentioned above that science has a problem with; probably partly because this ultra refined energy cannot be calibrated or made visible. However, nowadays there are such electronic devices that will confirm the existence of such immaterial puissance. On-line: James Oschman - Energy Medicine. As mentioned above: Be taken blindfolded into a prison and then into a cathedral and you will feel the difference in *Chi* - the more ethereal the essence, the more potent.

THE LORD'S PRAYER:

In recent years, since 1928 in fact, The King James Version of The Lord's Prayer (circa 1611) has been uttered in a fashion that, regrettably, has but all destroyed its mystical meaning. Only by changing a few words here and there, the deeper significance of this almost ineffable prayer has been bastardised to fit into the present-day vernacular - a vernacular generally devoid of the deeper and more profound dignity, beauty, grace and essential mystery that our present-day language cannot provide and also to help direct the mind and the heart to a loftier realm.

Originally it was a United States decision to change some of these words to simplify, thinking wrongly in my opinion, to appeal more to the average man and woman. This cheap alteration travelled into the United Kingdom and elsewhere and adopted for the same or similar reasons to align with the clergy's way of thinking in the U.S.A. and thus, it was adopted everywhere - similar to an update we all have to suffer and allow computer-wise... not always for the better!

To undertake such a fundamental change - they, the churchmen thinking that the changes were only slight but not realising that the alterations of important original chosen words were meant to uplift the mind and heart unto a higher realm, whatever and wherever that is! The way the Prayer is recited today is really almost meaningless because it has changed fundamentally.

Our Father*, which art in Heaven

Hallowed be Thy name

Thy kingdom come, Thy will be done

in Earth, as it is in Heaven.

Give us this day our daily bread,

and forgive us our trespasses,

as we forgive those who trespass against us;

and lead us not into temptation,

but deliver us from evil.

[For Thine is the kingdom,

the power and the glory

for ever and ever.] Amen.

*The Prayer begins: Our Father. In this way signifying the architect of creation.

* God-head: ………………..ditto……………………….

The words underlined in The Lord's Prayer, have been substituted with the words (from top to bottom): Who; Yours; Your; Your; on; Yours.

The first substitution of 'Who' for 'Which' generates the grave misunderstanding of envisaging a personage as a God-head*. It does not allow the imagination to expand and to atomise into many directions unfettered. In this way the mind is disallowed to interpret the thought and the feeling triggered by the recitation of the Prayer.

The 'Which' when read, allows an ethereal elevated understanding. The 'Who' at this place in the Prayer does not allow this boundless expansion of the Mind's imagination and thus the opening-out of the emotions of the Heart.

The second substitution 'Your' for 'Thy', generates the same idea of addressing the Prayer to a personage; so too, the third and the forth substitutions: 'Your' for 'Thy'.

The fifth substitution of 'on' for 'in', changes the subtle meanings of The Prayer absolutely. By applying the word 'on' at this position within The Prayer, the image of The Earth and its inhabitants is conjured-up, and a separation is automatically established between Heaven and Earth. When applying the word 'in' at this place in The Prayer, the wider vision of Heaven potentially within all that is mundane in all Earthly matters is perceived - thus, no particular thought of separation is engendered within the context of this section of The Prayer.

The sixth substitution 'Yours' for 'Thine' evokes again a personage to whom the Prayer is addressed - though these last three lines were added later ?

Confidentially, for many of us, the 'But' in this Prayer gives rise to possible incomprehension. This word may just be understood at this place within the text as: Though we humans struggle to keep an orderly and moral life, we must avoid at all costs being seduced into the mundane influences to which we are all subject and mistake them for the Truth. These influences may take us to evil places, away from the Power and the Glory of Heaven - Heaven for many, being the true reality!

*George Bernard Shaw (1856-1950): "Beware of the man whose God is in the skies".

Though to be fair, some people might say: 'tis better to recite the Prayer in whatever form it is in, than not recite it at all!

The King James Version may be deemed Masculine and the changes that took place in the 20th Century may be deemed Feminine. In the epoch following The 1st World War and to the present day, the lowest common denominator only, seems all to have mattered, and so the bending-over backwards to please the demos, the masses, led by the so called 'educated classes' has watered-down everything that has value and gravity. It is the present-day scientific obsession to Prove everything until the spirit of the object under examination has all but disappeared leaving a sterile shell - it is the shell we believe-in nowadays (Feminine - Proof).

This does not denigrate the Feminine, but without the Masculine wider view and influence, the feminine becomes condensed, and suffocates in its own inertia.

Taking the matter of word meanings further; entering the present 21st century, many words are losing their real meaning as the demos slides from the gutter and thence into the sewer. Instead of raising our aspirations in the way of improving ourselves in different life levels, we tend to concentrate on bettering ourselves (which is admirable) with external activities such as with Sports; Video Games and Gambling and more. Indeed if we take sporting activities as an example, sadly it rarely occurs to most of the athletes and the aspiring athletes, that improvement and achievement of self also means the changing of ourselves for the better in the way we carry ourselves and in the way we speak, write, communicate and in the way we show our civility and how we exercise good-manners – not to mention the essential development of the important but neglected spiritual aspects of our lives; probably the most important all-embracing subject of all.

It seems that only ugliness with all its foul human habits has and is rewarded. The slovenly way we apply words indicates the state of sleep that we seem all to be subject-to. Mum in instead of Mother. Mum is a private word used within the family unit. The letter T seems to be missing in the language: daugh-er instead of daughter. The letter G seems at times to be missing: It's rainin' for raining. The word kid for child. A kid is a baby goat. Shocking examples to the very young. There is much more of course, but so that I may keep my sense of balance and not suffer the incandescence of Rage. [Rage a Sanskrit word i.e. *Ragas* - vigour/energy/movement] as opposed to: Tame [Tame a Sanskrit word i.e. *Tamas* - quietude/peace/stillness].

Yes, language evolves, but there needs to be an articulate and a tasteful standard that disallows destruction of our languages.

THE CHURCH

With the especial ethos crushing our present-day society. It, society is suffering the obsession - mostly imposed on it - to establish subjective proof of the veracity of the details (a Feminine attribute that has its rightful place in the order of things) defining all the departments of life - like everything must be explained to the umpteenth degree - as we are forced to absorb, a sort of madness, imposed on us all in the way of being subject to the weight of laws, that have been passed and are being passed by government to the point whence most of us, in subtle ways, are experiencing now a state of derangement and confusion. Laws are being passed wholesale: law after law after law after law. We are being strangled by government but in truth this reflects the excessive guile of The Demos as defective Homo sapiens - us!

This wholesale passing of laws by our government is also a European governmental obsession. These bombardment of laws imposed on us from without, are really aspects of science of the present day that calculates via statistics and logic what it thinks society needs to allow it [society] to function without friction; and yet paradoxically they, the laws, generate resistance in their application when implemented.

In truth we have become so fearful of life's vicissitudes, that we apply aspects of science to resolve and to explain everything - which is: The New Church in fact, and it is not working as it is meant as it supplies only half the answers to life's conundrums.

In the present age, so many of our difficulties with much of the stress we suffer in our lives are the results of the ugly and uncontrollable tentacles of certain aspects of science penetrating their way into every crevice of life with their corrosive effects, in that it [science] does not allow for spontaneity, common sense, the bigger issue, freedom of spirit: 'blue sky thinking'. (Matters of the Masculine gender).

Not so long ago - one hundred years plus - we were still under the thrall of The Church (Masculine). In the times and issues of the past, religious dogma and doctrine dictated how to be, how to live and how to behave. The Church was dominant in all departments of life. Actually, the process of change to the more Secular ethos began, arguably, about the beginning of The Industrial Revolution (circa 1823) and onwards (Feminine). Science as we know it was then in its infancy.

A rational change was indeed required in our lives as individuals and as assemblages, but we have moved from one extreme to the other within this short time period of one hundred and fifty years plus. This new way, 'in extremis' has utilised the scientific approach.

Whereas for several thousand years, religion, superstition and 'fear of the unknown' were dominating the behaviour, mores and actions of a given People (Masculine), nowadays, we suffer under the opposite extreme in that our secular lives (Feminine) cause us to to run in circles, searching and searching for a better life, but in this way, we may or we will, all of us fall into a void and disappear, because we have forgotten, to our obvious detriment, the unseen and the miraculous in creation (Masculine).

'......further to our detriment, because certain aspects of science and scientific attitudes being far too cerebral and thereby sterile in practice, have embarked upon out of control experimentation with the natural world with dangerous consequences especially with agriculture. We do not question the energetic unseen effects that will, in time, manifest, because we did not, do not, see the bigger picture. That is, the rarefied ill-effects of playing loose with the 'order of things' whilst not understanding their place in nature, their place in creation. We love to interfere: what a mess the world is in!

In addition, science (Feminine: Proof) at its worst, has influenced us all, usually insidiously, in that we have been led to believe life as just a conglomeration of chemicals - the most appalling and damaging mistake of the way of thinking in the present-day. The sacredness and the mystery of life (Masculine: Truth) has nearly been squeezed into oblivion, bringing confusion into all the compartments of existence, as has already been mentioned above. It is no wonder why there exists now, so much neurosis, and consequent psychosis, as well as illness compared to times past.

How splendid our Societies would be if they understood the meaning of gender as conveyed within this Book; if for instance the brilliance of the scientific method of the present day were moderated by a sensitive comprehension of the hidden and sublime creative powers driving the marvel of aliveness.

We may then adopt easily what is taught in the Hindu Scriptures: Infusion with a *Sattvic* ethos. *Sattva* is the word given to 'The Middle Way' whose meaning is: living life in moderation, wholesomeness and fullness. **See below:**

This way or The Way of the Tao in fact, is the way of not living with and in extremes of any kind - neither too much nor too little - and thus: engendering splendid human behaviour. Much of the understanding of the contents of this Book between the Masculine and the Feminine may assist this process of moderation and fairness.

Hindu Esoteric Tradition teaches that there are these three characteristic forces in creation: Ragas, Tamas and Sattva as stated above. As mentioned above, the Sattvic third force is present when Ragas (rage) and Tamas (tame) are in equilibrium. We may deduce from the word Sattva, our word: satisfaction.

Thus, we have: Active (Ragas), Passive (Tamas) and Neutral (Sattva). These are the names of the three fundamental forces in nature in all things manifest, and in those notions about to become manifest: Male = Ragas; Female = Tamas; Sattva = equals child or the coming into being of something new as a result of the mingling of their other two gender forces.

Further: Ragas may represent the extreme of Heaven's Force but raw and as yet impractical, and Tamas may represent the extreme of Earth's Force with its excessive gravitation and virtually no release. Each Force needs the other to bring into being that which may be called normal and experienced as normal because both forces make to balance each other. The ways of Sattva equals perfection or near perfection because Ragas and Tamas are now in each other's thrall. Extreme Force of Heaven gives rise to aggression, in-ordinance and Rage (Ragas/Yang). Extreme Force of Earth produces inertia, torpidity and slovenliness (Tamas/Yin).

The reader may now be able to see these Forces in action in life as they - the readers - visualise hundreds of examples of extremes in events that have occurred and their accursed results, and other examples of the excellent outcomes of the balanced expression of the these Forces.

'......OUT OF THE BOWELS
OF THE TEXTS ABOVE;
ADDITIONAL ISSUES FOLLOW:

It may be understood much better now why there seem always to be two sides to an issue and a subject - they are understood better when the divisions are marked as either Masculine or as Feminine both in Time and in Space, both in Earth and in Heaven, both in Yin and in Yang, both in the Temporal and in the Ethereal.

The scientific method is applied to the workings of our law courts. In many cases this is a good thing, and in others, it makes the carrying-out of the law appear to be incompetent.

We may take the Court shenanigans in The United Kingdom regarding the case of one, a Farmer protecting his property for the umpteenth time, and doing the public a great service, by executing an intruder within his property (a known felon) and public enemy number one anyway, and his [The Farmer] serving time in Her Majesty's Prison for the reward to his natural and normal human re-action to this low-life, the same low-life who had burgled his property at times previously.

The guilty verdict of the Court handed down to the Farmer and the subsequent prison sentence was his payment to nullify his misdeed - misdeed as interpreted by the Court. The Farmer's re-action in shooting dead the criminal intruder who was uninvited and trespassing within his property, and had carried-out the same burgling deed in earlier times, was sufficient, whilst the Farmer was present within his property, to engender that kind of re- action - protecting his house and himself. This ugly event of trespass inducing the action of the owner of his now vulnerable property to punish the trespasser, would in most countries of the world be applauded as self-preservation dictates.

With human-beings who possess a strong sense of justice and who are generally upright in their way of living would consider the actions of the defendant to be normal. The Law is meant to protect the innocent and to defend those who have suffered and are suffering the felonies of others.

The implementation of the law outlined above, may be deemed a Feminine aspect of creation (adhering to the letter). The law as it should have been interpreted in this case should be a Sentence of so many months in prison, but the actual carrying-out of this punishment suspended indefinitely.   This would follow the Masculine aspect of creation (truth, common-sense, and the seeing of The Bigger Picture).

HEALTH & SAFETY LEGISLATION:

Many good changes have come about with the care and the responsibilities this type of legislation that has procured those needed rules and regulations governing, for instance, a building-sight. The wearing of coloured protective clothing that shows that a particular group, belonging to a given organisation, may be trusted as such, because wearing the same coded colour clothing gives the impression of unity and cohesion away from casualness and therefore slovenliness.

Being unfree to explore aspects of existence however, in other particular walks of life, because of restricting legislation, has to damage spontaneity and dare, especially when the young are involved.

Adhering to the 'letter of the law' no matter how rigid is a Feminine aspect, and the spontaneity to, and the re-action to life's challenges is a Masculine aspect, as per the conveyances of this Book.

Being free to explore, and to learn by error (that is a human condition), is being squeezed out of existence; and so for us older generation, we can only mourn the passing of life's thrills that the young will not be able to experience fully as we did when we were young.

This may result in the growth of less able, but more feeble males and females being unable to suffer life's abundant 'knocks' that existence creates to help cultivate maturity within us... to make us stronger.

This could have detrimental effects on modern humanity because of the decline in the capacity for modern humans to cope with life's vicissitudes, as is already happening - 'the snowflake generation' - so called!

GENETICALLY MODIFIED VEGETATION

Science has, and scientists have worked wonders in respect to the strengthening of vegetation against the onslaught of creatures that are pestilential. In addition, the longer shelf-life they now inherently have the more convenient they are to industry and in storage and therefore in money saving.

The forfeit to this progress (progress: so called) as yet not completely understood, and as George Oshawa said: "What has a front, has a back", could be ghastly in the extreme. The interfered-with plants for human consumption and those interfered-with plants consumed by animals - animals that we as humans eat, will, with little doubt have painful consequences for us as the future unfolds (just as living with radio-waves, micro-waves and WIFIs' that every household possess now and the adverse effects these must have on us yet to manifest).

The adverse 'energetic' effects, presently barely observable will cause consternation amongst the responsible and caring people around us; sufficient to create a political movement that must act to halt the potential presently unseen and unfelt effects of this run- away technology of the present-day.

The science that underlies G.M. Products is sound and is deemed Feminine (Proof). Proof is the present-day ethos that must record every detail until the subject under scrutiny becomes sterile and barren.

The dire consequences of this science yet to manifest fully is deemed Masculine (Truth) in the horrible effects to come. That is, the 'energetic' signs, and the 'bigger picture' not yet obvious, so subtle, will reveal itself eventually to show the unrepairable damage to us as humans and to the soil which nourishes vegetation.

In time of course, we will witness excuses and lies told by those still responsible for damaging and even destroying those things that were always considered normal and health- giving when what is left to consume will prospectively be inimical to health and inimical to wholesome living.

It does not have to be this way. There are many fine and upright human-beings forming a moving stream that is against the current ethos of this present sterile penetration into things that should remain sacred and untouchable - 'if it ain't broke, then don't try to fix it'!

These more sensitive people, perhaps a silent majority, appreciate and respect all aspects of the Yin and the Yang of creation. Ethics being the operative word here and applied to all the realms of life by those who enjoy awareness of the gifts of the Earth and who intuitively know how not to abuse it.

THE SECULAR INQUISITION

In the present incomparable and confused age in which we live, and because very little is understood due to the complexities that certain aspects of science has wrought upon us, its rationale has disallowed the embracement of 'The Bigger Picture' and thus, we are unable to enjoy the spontaneity and freedoms we, until recently took for granted - the present scientific ethos being one that is limited because of its obsession with minutiae.

Alas, the present-day psychosis to meddle in all departments of life reflects the growing problem of science to rationalise all aspects of the spectacular diversity of life and thus imagination and spontaneity required for many of these aspects is hampered.

Because we as the people have become very fearful of life's vicissitudes, our governments use secular scientific methods to control us/society more and more - just be aware of the hundreds of laws being passed by government to rein us in day-in, day-out. However, these laws reflect the guile of human-behaviour - it is us, the people, who are culpable. We try to change everything outside of us by complaint, never realising that the outside reflects in the inside. It is we as individuals who need the change, if we want a better world!

The Spanish Inquisition circa 1423 A.D., managed to control its population on pain of death or at least by fundamental conversion and pretty well succeeded - threats were more directed to the suffering of physical pain. The difference with today's (Secular) Inquisition is that we are being murdered by restrictive laws that drive most of us to suffer modern-day neurosis - more towards mental/psychological pain. Who isn't on some kind of nostrum to keep him/her from suffering the present-day stresses?

We have become Worriers (Worriers: could be a new word for homo-sapiens). Of course, ideally, we should be Warriors, though this

68

is difficult within the present epoch of modern humanity and with the State Governments controlling us more and more by the minute - controlling us successfully by applying brilliant scientific methods to do so.

Nothing now must be left to chance as to the vagaries of life, but to be fair, as the populations of the world become more cunning and treacherous, then more laws have to be passed to control them/us!

One day perhaps our scientists will respect and have time to investigate the rarefied and the more ethereal aspects of a given subject - these are the energies that usually evade our scientific machines that calibrate all and sundry - but they may be measured and acknowledged as equally in importance as the material manifestations that are the ones always acknowledged because they of course may be calibrated.

We are fed information that is verified and therefore may be accurate on one level, but that information will have hidden aspects, initially unmeasured that will have different consequences modifying the original truth; the veracity of that information. For instance, the mists of ethereal energies, as mentioned above, may assist us to perceive that it is the Earth that rotates around the Sun, whilst the obvious more mundane elements allow us actually to witness the Sun rotating around the Earth. Two truths, one Masculine, the other one Feminine.

If the brilliance of present-day science allows itself to enjoy, to acknowledge two truths, but of different energetic qualities, then it will be wholesome in its experimentation and will understand the effects of these experiments on different levels that may or may not damage life.

After-all, most of us know that so many moments of discovery happen by revelation - a eureka moment! Intuition must be allowed to be part of the discovery process.

Einstein said: "Science without religion is lame; religion without science is blind".

Einstein also said: "Imagination [Masculine] is more important than knowledge.

Knowledge [Feminine] is limited. Imagination encircles the world".

From Page 7:

This extraordinary period of approx 300 years under the Saxon kings in England that so determined our insensitivity to the masculine and to the feminine division in many departments of life and especially so, in the spoken language of that epoch, may be explained for two major reasons, in addition to the points proffered on page 7. One: Because of the integration, at that time, of the two languages French and Old English that generated some linguistic difficulties, and Two: A spiritual and theological problem that was uppermost in the minds of the hierarchical clergy of the Catholic Church, all within that epoch.

In many religious traditions of the world, the Sun and the Moon were/are considered as masculine for the Sun and feminine for the Moon. This basic doctrine determined the gender value of nouns and adjectives in most languages with their nominated masculine and feminine character. However, this tradition did not always stand-up to basic scientific* scrutiny. The reality on a certain level was/is that the Moon has, and manifests certain masculine traits, and with the Sun, certain of its traits reveal feminine attributes.

This way of thinking engendered some confusion to the Anglo-Saxon mind and so our language (English) was driven to become neutered over that 300 year period such, as its words, especially nouns and adjectives did not reflect gender division and so the esoteric character of words would yield no argument in this complex subject.

*Rudimentary Science as it was then.

"The person who takes medicine must recover twice. Once from the disease and once from the medicine."

Willaim Osler, MD

Sir William Golding
regarding women

I think women are foolish to pretend they are equal to men, they are far superior and always have been. Whatever you give a woman, she will make it greater. If you give her sperm, she'll give you a baby. If you give her a house, she'll give you a home. If you give her groceries, she'll give you a meal. If you give her a smile, she'll give you her heart. She multiplies and enlarges what is given to her. So, if you give her any crap, be ready to receive a ton of shit!

HOW IT ALL STARTED

Below, is an additional legend to supply the key to unlock this oxymoron of both the simplicity of the concepts of the texts above, and simultaneously, the almost unsolvable complications that arise with this whole abstruse subject. The texts below are likened to The Big Bang theory as promulgated by astronomers and physicists alike, but another dimension is added here which is both masculine and feminine and this added dimension is totally absent within the theories as taught by these eminent professionals.

The Great Architect, The Creator, makes himself known through His emanations - emanations that spread-out in all directions simultaneously, and they do so initially from a Point in Space (Heaven) and this, to animate all material things and to innervate all possible life-forms from within these very emanations assuming that all material things came into being simultaneously within these emanations? This initial overwhelming force of energy is centrifugal in nature and is deemed masculine in character whilst everything made of matter is deemed feminine and is therefore centripetal in nature. Both energy and matter are irresistibly attracted to each other in myriad combinations and one cannot manifest without the other. Interestingly, this idea tallies with The Big Bang Theory.

Inside these emanations therefore, is the full spectrum of all that is temporal, but, from the rarified to the densest. The rarefied material is closest to the origin-point and the more dense material is away from this origin-point. The more dense matter is, the more laws, the more complications tend to present. Therefore His presence wanes with every descending level of material diversification - this is because His initial purity has to be compromised with every descending level as material strictures become stronger with their stifling addiction to detail. Just as an initial explosion weakens as its effects move away from its centre - inertia takes-over and the consequences good and bad follow-on.

Indeed, as expressed above, is it possible to call every level of descent a calibrated lowering of puissance from Heaven and then to Earth? This is generally how we humans see these Heaven/Earth relationships. From the refined to the basest of the mundane - bearing in mind that this relationship is the one only that may manifest for us which is of the highest and refined, to the lowest and depraved. Such has consequences and repercussions in all departments of life as we experience them in our living existence!

For the sake of simplicity, even though the energy of heat, light and consciousness emanates from One Point in the universe and is therefore centrifugal in nature, it behoves us to imagine this holy force as descending, as it [heat, light and consciousness] intermingles with each material level of descent and more so as it is irresistibly attracted to the material things on all levels as it approaches Earth (matter) or to The Earth? Heaven attracts Earth, and Earth attracts Heaven, just as with man (Yang) and woman (yin). Traditionally, Heaven (Yang) is masculine and Earth (Yin) is feminine.

Yet, the statements made in the earlier paragraphs rather than the one above, imply that material and temporal things already existed and were ready to receive the Life-Force of Heaven to be woken-up and utilised for good, and even for holy purposes - this includes physical matter and flesh !

All material things, if they existed in Space before The Creator's Descent, would be made of dust, gas and ice and any other form of material all floating aimlessly in Space before the kiss of life from The One, in and of Heaven.

Yet it could be argued that within His Descent all this physical phenomena came out of His emanations, and therefore pre-existed, in concept at least, and with each descent a coalescence of these materials formed Suns and Planets and therefore eventually life-forms as they were intermingled with His life-force.

Astronomically speaking, in Space, there is no up and down, north and south, or side to side as terms we normally employ to calibrate geometrically all earthly matters. Therefore, the first gargantuan energy explosion [implosion before explosion in fact] as expounded above and spreading-out circularly, wave after wave would be better to convert within our minds, one of linear Descent of energy and matter as already employed in the texts above - thus, the meanings of these texts may then be understood in betterment.

THE REST IS HISTORY !

www.ingramcontent.com/pod-product-compliance
Lightning Source LLC
Chambersburg PA
CBHW032102020426
42335CB00011B/463